THE QUEEN CODE

Reigning and Ruling your Personal Queendom

By: Tonisha L. Dawson

ISBN-13:978-1530617937

ISBN-10: 1530617936

Tonishadawson.com

lovetherapies@gmail.com

Disclaimer: The author of this book has put together this work for the purpose of self-help. The author makes no guarantees or promises of results and will not be held liable for loss or damages. This work does not represent the expert opinion of a Physician, Psychologist, or Psychiatrist and if the reader is in need of expert help, the author encourages the reader to seek a professional for services needed.

The Queen Code

About the Author

Tonisha Dawson has been leading and helping people to change their lives for over 15 years. She teaches monthly course studies on life changing topics, runs and interactive life coaching group, and also helps women to rebuild and regain their self-esteem through various methods that she has acquired over the years. As she continued to move forward she began to realize through her own personal experiences that stress, negativity, the power of thought and the everyday wiles of daily living contribute to our physical and emotional ailments, as well as our manifested realities. With this epiphany she incorporated the power of meditation, the healing of Reiki and the principles of metaphysics into her reptoire. Using the skills and the services that she has acquired and refined over the years, she creatively unifies her training to customize treatments and teachings for those in need. Tonisha Dawson attended the University of Metaphysics for her Masters Degree, holds a Bachelors in Holistic Life Coaching, and is a Certified Reiki Master, she also holds a Certification from the National Association of Christian Counseling (NACC) as a certified Spiritual Advisor.

Table of Contents

Introduction

<u>Introduction</u>

As Women, there are a host of things that we go through on a daily, weekly, monthly and even yearly basis. We are the pillars, the rock and the backbone of our families. Our children, spouses, and even parents may rely on us to do the virtually impossible, and we meet these needs with ease. You may also be on the other end of the spectrum and forgo the family life but are very active and acclimated to the business world, in this case you may have even more pressure as you adapt to the intense demands of Corporate America or the needs of your own business. It can be super difficult to adjust to the male dominated world of business or just as stressful bending to the needs of your family, whichever route that you are traveling upon, the pressure is definitely on to perform at a very high level.

We are virtually Superwomen! Women have amazing powers of intuition, discernment, nurturing, persuasion, passion, communication and attraction. These are all extremely positive attributes and with all of this extreme poweress, we have to be very careful to use our powers for good and not evil. As cliché as this may sound, it is the absolute truth. Everything in life is two sides of the same coin and we have the capacity to operate in one or the other in any given moment. As amazing as the above mentioned attributes that you possess are, you will have to be just as cautious and refrain from having your intuition and discernment turn into paranoia, your nurturing to turn into nagging, your persuasion to evolve into manipulation, your passion to grow into reckless emotions, your communication to backslide into gossip and idle conversation and your attraction to move into promiscuity or reckless abandonment.

This is where the "true" work on our behalf lies. It is very easy for us to operate in a negative polarity, simply because it takes immense inner and spiritual work to rise above the ego part of ourselves. We are essentially *two* beings in every moment. A positive and a negative, a Higher Self or God and Ego or Flesh. Whichever one that you "feed" or act in the majority, will be the most prevalent in your life. What we need to modify as women is learning how to act in our power majority of the time and leave your nemesis at the door! This nemesis is "the enemy of me" It is the part of yourself that has the potential to hold you back from your success and your innermost desires. It is allowing emotional baggage and pain from your past to yank you back from your promising future. It is the petty and menial arguments and faulty perceptions. It is ANY and EVERYTHING about you that keeps you stagnated and stuck in your current position or situation.

In the pages that follow, we are going to delve deeper into these amazing and potent powers that we as women possess as well as how to expand them and utilize them for our benefit. We will also explore the opposite side of our poweress and discover those things that have hindered us in our progression toward a successful future. The keys that are put forth in this power packed read will surely set your path ablaze toward a promising future, whether it be in your career, relationship, your children, and everything in between!

The Queen Code

If you are ready to see "real "change in your life and the lives around you, join me in this enlightening journey of regaining your positive power, reigning supreme, and Embracing Your Queendom!

1
<u>The Gifts (Untapped Power)</u>

Since the absolute beginning of time women have possessed many, many powers that enable us in short, to pretty much do and achieve whatever we will. These gifts are not by accident or by chance. Women were created to be the very vessels to birth new life, dreams and experiences into this world, not only physically but we exhibit this same power spiritually as well. This is why it is of upmost importance how we decide to wield this power.

Power that is not focused correctly can be catastrophic and when the purpose of something is unknown, destruction is inevitable.

This is where many of you dwell. Your power, because of its incorrect focus has produced catastrophic results for you, OR you have not truly understood the purpose of your power and therefore have destroyed opportunities, relationships, and possibly your careers as a result of.

This power that lies on the inside of us can yield AMAZING results if utilized correctly and in the correct circumstances. This power can propel you from Point A to Point B, and this power can lead you straight down the waterfall of success if you would allow.

Have you ever been in a room full of people and that ONE woman walked in and stood out above the rest? I think we have all been in this situation at one point or another and wondered silently to ourselves "How does she do it"? What is it that this particular woman is doing that is *different* from what everyone else is doing? Yes, we can attribute it to how she may be dressed, her physical beauty, a certain hairstyle or her makeup choice, but inside, we *know* that it is deeper than that. What this woman displays is *her personal power,* her authority over herself and her personal kingdom. She knows what this power is and more importantly she knows how to utilize it for her benefit.

This is the energy that you want to exude when walking into a room, entering a business meeting or sitting down for interviews. This is the inner glow and confidence that you want others, not only to see, but to also *"feel"* while they are in your presence.

This is the very energy that will change a No into a Yes! A maybe into a definitely and uncertainty into absolute certainty! This energy is the catalyst to tip you over the edge into the pool of success!

There are many facets to this energy and if you unify them effectively you will create a cocktail of positive explosion for your life. Many women, because of our heightened emotions, can fall into ruts of negativity, uncertainty, depression, insecurity, failure, instability and the list can continue on, but again, as I stated in earlier text, everything has its complete opposite and

YOU decide which one you will operate in at any given moment. Everyday life's circumstances allow us to see certain aspects of ourselves that we may not readily notice and we have the choice to choose at that very moment to utilize that opportunity to grow or stay stagnated. This is powerful, because it is God's job to reveal to us WHO we truly are and once we recognize who we are, we are to make the necessary adjustments to grow past that person in any given state. The Universe uses life's situations and circumstances to reveal to us the TRUE US! Many of you look at certain situations in your life with an unhealthy perspective. These situations were divinely orchestrated to attract themselves to you for the purpose of growth. It is up to you to decide WHAT you are going to do and WHO you are going to be once the situation arises. This is going to be where we begin our work. We need to first and foremost decide *who* we want to be and how we want to be perceived. This answer is going to differ based on what you desire as well as personal preferences and what you would like to achieve. I will use myself as an example, I do not judge behavior in general, my rule of thumb is that you have to make the decisions that are best for you, however, I do begin to look at behavior if it goes contrary to what you say that you desire. For example, if you desire a true mate, it would be in your best interest not to try to attain a job at the local strip club. A true mate may not respect your line of work and his presence mays be kept away from you. In my personal case, I have always wanted to help people, encourage them, write books and become a life coach and as many opportunities that were presented to me to release my integrity or to hurt someone because they had hurt me, I declined them all because I knew that in my line of work I had to talk the talk but I would also have to walk the walk and practice what I preached. This behavior was best for my particular path, and you will have to pick the path that will work best for your life and what you would like to do with it. This is going to be very important as you embark upon your future.

This is exactly where utilizing our amazing gifts will come into effect. If used correctly, they will assist us in making the best possible decisions for our future and ultimately our success. Let's talk more about these awesome gifts before we go any further.

The first gift that I would like to bring to light is our beautiful gift of INTUITION. Let's break ground with this, women were created differently than men and our energy is completely different as well. If you have ever heard of the concept Yin and Yang this is the absolute perfect example of it. Women are Yin (female energy) and men are Yang (Male energy) completely equal and opposite. Let me explain to you a little bit about the difference in these energies. Yin, is a very cool, water based energy that is intuitive and fluid and moves like the rippling of the waves in water. It is the energy that is subtle, serene, pliable and free spirited. It draws in and is alluring and magnetic. Magnetism is the way that this energy moves. Magnets do not force anything, magnets pull in and attract. This is the awesome energy that women possess! This energy moves with the waxes and wanes of the moon and even our menstrual cycles are controlled by it. It is meant to cool things down, not to amp things up and the Yin energy uses a different type of energy to get things done. It does not have to force anything, things are attracted and magnetized to it. Things are drawn in, not by force but by allure. One of the more powerful traits of this energy is its intuitive abilities. Women were created to be the intuits, the feelers and the foreseers of their families and we have done a great job with this. We are "sense" based and we can feel and intuit when things are off or going wrong for our family. This is a tremendous gift to possess. Imagine the good that this gift can bring to you and your home. The mere fact that you can *feel* when something is off in your life or the lives around you can be of extreme assistance to someone in need. Begin to apply this gift to your life, if you have not begun already, it will surely take your life to new heights. The key to activating this gift is to get in touch with your Inner Higher Self, Your Higher Power, God and The Holy Spirit. This is the inner part of you that hears and knows everything, even things that have not yet occurred naturally. Have you ever been thinking about someone, and your phone rings or you receive a text and it's from the very person you were thinking about? This is a prime example of your intuition at work in your life, however it lacks guidance. The important point is to learn to use it at will and not solely by chance. The way that you can begin to do this is by prayer, meditation and quieting your mind so that your Spirit can speak to you and you actually *hear* It. Your Spirit is speaking to you at ALL times, but many times the wiles of life, TV, background noise, petty arguments, ego and a host of other things speak over it and drown out the small still voice of God that is alerting you of things to come. The more you assert yourself to these practices, the stronger this gift will become and the more you will be able to implement it effectively in your life for you and your family.

If this is all new to you, you may not be educated in how to pray or to meditate which makes it easier to hear this soft voice. I will give you a few techniques for this. We will begin with prayer.

Many people are confused as to what "prayer" truly is. Prayer, contrary to popular belief, is not a petition to

God for him to meet our needs and desires. Many, when they think of prayer, think of something they saw on TV, or even more specifically something they saw in a church service. This does not necessarily brand it to be true or even effective for that matter. *True Prayer* is believing in your heart, with every part of your being that what you desire is making its way to you. *True Prayer* is thanking God that what you desire in your heart, He has already done for you and you are simply waiting on the physical manifestation of it. Prayer is not begging God to save the day for you or to help you out of a situation, the power that you need to get out of any situation already lies within you NOW at this very moment, this is why Prayer is merely being thankful that it is ALREADY done. Once you have completed this prayer, your next step is to *act as if* whatever you desire has already made its way to you. This is the absolute epitome of FAITH. Faith is believing in what is not yet seen. Your faith and your belief unified will cause your manifestations to occur at a much speedier rate.

Meditation is a somewhat different. Meditation is the practice of quieting the mind. It is becoming completely still and allowing Your Higher Self to rise up and become strong. It is in this complete stillness that dreams, visions, inspired ideas and that small voice will make its way known to you. The practice of meditation has been around for thousands of years, Monks, Buddhists and even Christians have taken an invested interest in this practice with phenomenal results but make no mistake, quieting the mind is not easy, it is an inner spiritual work. It is the equivalent of attempting to get a two-year old to sit still for 20 minutes without moving, this is virtually impossible without consistent training and this is what you will have to do to get your mind on the right track. The key in meditation is to clear your mind of ANY thoughts and focus on your breathing. The moment that a thought trails into your mind, your job is to immediately dismiss it and begin to focus on your breathing once again. This sounds super easy however you will find that it is quite difficult to keep your mind free of any thoughts. Random thoughts will begin to flow into your mind, how Dunkin Donuts forgot the cream in your coffee, your child's parent teacher meeting, if you remembered to go to the bank, what your mother said to you earlier, your responsibilities for the day and the list will go on and on, your job is to immediately shed the thoughts and refocus on your breathing. In the beginning this may seem difficult, but I can assure you that if you keep it up, it will become easier and easier over time. Try to start off small... two minutes at first, time yourself, then up your timing minute by minute until you can get yourself up to about ten minutes undisturbed by thoughts. Ten minutes undisturbed by thoughts is ample time for your Higher Spirit to be able to relay a message to you. Over a period of time, you will be able to increase your meditation time to about 30 minutes, an hour or even longer periods, and you will undoubtedly get better with practice. This is where your intuition will reach new heights!

There is also another form of meditation and this method is called Visualizations. This is a technique where you close your eyes and "see" or imagine your life as you would like it to be and it is an awesome catalyst for manifestation. Understand, the subconscious mind does not know the difference between what is real or imagined so it goes to immediate spiritual work drawing your desires in for you. It uses the fastest, speediest way… a way that we may not see, nor understand, to bring our innermost prayers and desires to us. This is why it is of uttermost importance to NEVER look at your natural circumstances as a point of reference. Natural circumstances have the ability to change on a whim based on the power of our subconscious minds and our intuition can alert us of things to come.

I have found that the ideal time for me to practice my visualizations are at night, right before I drift off to sleep. This works best for me because the subconscious is still active while you are asleep and I enjoy the fact that my visualizations are done the moment before my conscious mind falls asleep. This causes my dreams to be more vivid, and my subconscious mind can work its fresh magic on magnetizing me while I am asleep. Some prefer to do their visualizations very early in the morning upon waking, as they feel that it will help them to start their day fresh, positive and recharged. Either way, the technique will profit results nonetheless.

The absolute best way to implement your visualizations is to *see* yourself having, being or doing whatever it is that you desire. The key is to see from YOUR perspective, from your eyes and your outlook. Many make the grave mistake of visualizing and watching themselves as in a scene from a movie, they are watching themselves from the outside looking in, or from an audience perspective. This is not correct! This tells the mind that you are watching someone else. You have to SEE it as though you are living it, as though *you* are doing it. This is the absolute best way to see results and to see them quickly.

These three methods will literally begin to raise your personal vibrations and help you to quiet your mind so that you will be able to hear Divinely inspired thoughts, Higher Self and Holy Spirit talking to you. The more you implement these techniques into your life, the more you will develop and amplify your intuition. Your intuition is like a muscle, the more you utilize it, the stronger it gets and is always at your disposal.

Another gift that we as women possess is the natural gift of nurturing. This is a gift that is inbred into our nature as women. There are a select few that may not exhibit this gift for various reasons, but as for the majority, this is a gift that lies in all of us. Women do an awesome job at nurturing, it is a part of our calling here on this earth and it is truly a huge part of our work in the world. When we try to fight or disown this gift, we are out of balance with a vital element of who we are. From the time that little girls are able to walk, talk and play, they find something to nurture, whether it be a favorite baby doll, a pet or a younger sibling. We want to help take care of something and this instinct only expands more so as we grow with age.

As women, we give life, create life and sustain life. It Is up to us and us alone whether a baby can be "born" into this world and survive. We require men's help, let's be clear, but the work to sustain life is done solely by us. We nurture, provide nourishment, feed, train, educate, rear and care for those around us in a very big way especially our children. This is a gift! We give of ourselves in such a way that sometimes we end up depleting ourselves. This is something that is done freely and naturally on our end, it is simply part of our blueprint. This gift causes us to have patience for those around us and also gives us the strength to pour into a life other than our own. We are the pillars of life, we make sure that everyone is fed, taken care of, clothed, soothed, healed, warm, nursed and the list goes on. The key here is to keep this all in a healthy balance, you do not want to give so much of yourself that you end up running on an empty tank, this will set major grounds for issue in the future. When you understand that this desire to help others is a natural part of your blueprint as a woman, it will be much easier to keep things in balance and in proper perspective. However, just because we have this awesome gift that lies on the inside of us does not mean that it is our role to help, assist, or to nurture every situation. This can cause problems for you and we will jump further into that later.

If you are a woman who does not nurture naturally, this is okay. Do not berate yourself about this, some women are better called for this than others based on genetic makeup and personality temperaments, but I would like you to dig deeper as to why you may be apprehensive in this area. There could be past hurts lurking in your past that pull the reigns in when you feel the urge to use this gift. I need you to understand that this gift is special, this gift grows and evolves the things around you, it encourages and uplifts others and this is undoubtedly your special offering to the world. Use it wisely!

The next very influential gift that we possess is the gift of Persuasion. In short, the true meaning of this word means; To prevail on a person to do something, as by advising or urging". It means to induce someone to believe by appealing to reason or understanding. It means simply... to convince. This is our power! We can use it at will. This power works in pretty much any circumstance and can propel you forward in life if you know how to wield it. The story of Adam and Eve was a prime example of this; Adam was created by God, and was instructed by God himself to refrain from eating the fruit from the tree in the center of the garden. Eve comes along, tricked by the serpent and literally convinced her husband, through logic and understanding, to eat the fruit that his Creator himself had told him not to eat. This is indeed some potent power! Women have an uncanny ability to convince and persuade people, especially men, to do pretty much anything. When we operate in *this* power, we showcase our subtle strength without being controlling and overbearing. This is an amazing gift to have and would do much good to begin to implement immediately! This gift alone can begin to change your life for the better, it's all about tapping into it. Tapping into this potent energy, will assist you in building new relationships, aid in maintaining the ones you have, facilitate networking, as well as moving the hand or the heart of your mate. What I want you to realize is that every woman does not tap into this power for many reasons... personality preferences, lack of understanding of it, ignorance of its presence, feeling incapable, etc. etc. But if you give it the opportunity, it can draw many wonderful experiences your way.

The best way to activate this gift is first and foremost by THINKING. Thinking is your gateway to persuasion. Contrary to popular belief, persuasion is not run by your emotions. A lot of women believe that persuasion is whining and nagging for what you want; this cannot be farther from the truth. Persuasion is using your logic/thinking coupled with your feminine wiles, your allure, and your inner knowing of a situation to sway or convince a decision. This starts by thinking. You cannot move anyone by inaccurate, invalid or questionable information, this will never work, and this is usually where our emotions will bring us. Emotions will cause you to present information that has nothing to do with logic and it will most definitely be perceived as questionable. When you bring information that is factual, in addition to your intuition and those feminine traits of seduction, you can sway just about ANYTHING! Remember as a woman to always bring truth and integrity to a situation, you do not want to use this gift for selfish gain, this is in no way MANIPULATION, which is an opposite polarity that we will delve into much deeper in the upcoming chapter. Presenting *truth* is a must and you will have already won half of the battle with this trait alone.

The second part of persuasion cannot be taught and it is unique to every woman, this brings us directly into our next gift; the gift of Attraction. The true meaning of attraction is one of absolute POWER! This means you possess; magnetic charm, and fascination. You are a person that draws, attracts, allures or entices, and one of the most important aspects of this definition, is that it is the electric or magnetic force that acts between oppositely charged bodies! Spiritually this means that something can be opposed to you or an idea and *can still* be magnetically attracted to you...this means that you can *win* no matter what! Women have this amazing gift of attraction and by attraction I am not merely speaking of the beauty in your face, or your physique I am talking about the magnetic allure that resides on the inside of you and it lives on the inside of each and every one of us. The most efficient way that this magnetic attraction is activated is by POSITIVITY! Positivity is the allure and the magnetic pull that can move ANY situation or circumstance in your favor. Positivity is the gateway for your success in persuasion and it is the most important catalyst to set your path on a successful one. Let's be very clear, NO ONE wants to be in the presence of a complaining, nagging, negative, pessimistic, unforgiving, petty, glass half full type of woman...I know this may sound harsh but it is the truth! People will detest your presence and you will only be tolerated at best. More on this in the following chapter. Now let's trail back up to my original point; The more that you can magnetize yourself with positivity and healthy emotions, more of the same will be attracted right back to you. This is spiritual law.

The next magnificent gift that I would like to shed light upon is our gift of Passion. I am not speaking of passion in the form of sexual desire, I am speaking on powerful and compelling emotion, strong feeling and desire. Women are blessed with this trait imbedded into our nature just like coded DNA. Women are emotional beings and although this has been painted as a negative, it is actually an extremely positive and powerful trait when used correctly. If this amazing gift is channeled and focused correctly, it contains huge manifestation abilities for your life. Emotions are the potent additive that supercharges your thoughts and brings them to fruition, without them, your thoughts will remain just words and images that ring through your mind with no true ability to manifest.

Emotions are key when it comes to creating for your life. They charge the atmosphere and begin to literally move and shift the minute particles that make up our universe and atmosphere ultimately shifting and moving situations and circumstances for you as well. Without the energy and vibrations of your emotions, your thoughts alone lack the capability of bringing your desires into physical form. In this sense you will have to be very careful, your emotions can also have an adverse effect on your life as well and we will most definitely explore this is our next chapter as well.

This passion that we possess is alluring. It causes people, places and things to be attracted to us at an energetic level! This by far supersedes the attraction we have because of our looks or personality...this passion attracts for us at a much deeper level. This passion can showcase through the things we love, activities that we take interest in, our sex life, our vibrancy, the love for our children, walking in your purpose in life, fulfilling your work in the world and things of this nature. Simply put, our passions almost always showcase (for lack of better terms) toward the things that we are passionate about. This is where you have to be careful; just because you are passionate about something, especially if it is in regards to something that you are upset about, you can also change your situation for the worse! Emotions are not a respecter of situations and they are surely not biased. They will assist you in manifesting whether it is positive or negative, the choice truly lies within you which way you are going to decide to tip the scale. You can pull things in based on these passions or you can keep them away. The choice is truly yours.

The last gift that we are going to open up, is our incredible gift of Communication. Women for the most part are great communicators, more so than the male species. We know how to express our feelings in words and paint an expressive picture to others as it relates to our thought processes. Some women are better at this than others for the simple fact of personality differences, but in general we have the gift of gab. This is due partly to the fact that we move between both sides of our brains, giving us the opportunity to access information from either side in any given moment, men did not inherit this ability. Men think with one side of the brain making them entirely more logical and less communicative. They do *have* this capability of expressing how they feel but they will usually opt out and forgo this option. Women are GREAT with this gift, we talk to our mothers, family members, best friends, acquaintances and we will share what is truly going on within us. We may not tell everyone, but we surely have a confidante or two that, at times, may receive an earful! What many women DO NOT realize is that this is one of the most powerful gifts we have! The Bible tells us that "Death and life are in the power of the tongue" It is from the words, confessions, and affirmations of our mouths that will change a situation for us. This gift is extremely important, this is why you have to monitor and control what you allow to come out of your mouth on any given occasion. THIS IS IMPORTANT! Words are spoken energy, and they are a very imperative part of your creation process. They literally create and form your world around you. Whatever you do not want to see manifest in your life…DO NOT SPEAK IT! I know that this is highly easier said than done, but I want to challenge you to challenge yourself. Work on your language and the seeds that come out of your mouth. Every thought that trails through your mind does not have to be entertained nor do you have to verbalize it. Once you verbalize, these seeds are emitted into the atmosphere and seek fervently to bring you what it is that you have confirmed with your words. Use this gift in your favor! Begin to speak life into your situation, positive affirmations and sincere and genuine words. These will surely change your life for the better. The more positivity you speak, the more your mind will begin to line up and your thoughts will begin to change as well. Once your thoughts change, your language will inevitably change and by default your life will begin to change for the better. This is also Spiritual Law. Work on it!

As we trail up and look over these significant gifts that we are blessed with, it truly shows us the power that lies on the inside of each and every one of us. It is totally up to you to decide whether you are going to tap into this power, the choice is yours! Will you begin to grow and cultivate these gifts that reside in you awaiting to be awakened or will you continue your life as it is, complaining and being tossed to and fro by the waves of life? These gifts alone provide us with the tools to succeed and become all that we are purposed to be. It will assist and propel us into a promising and successful future.

As we move down into our next chapter, I will shed light on the opposite end of the gifts and what these may look like.

2

<u>Opposite Polarity (The Other Side)</u>

As we have explored the above-mentioned gifts and the positivity that it will bring to your life, we also have to explore its counterparts and how we may have been operating on the opposite end of our gifting and causing chaos and stress in our lives. As I mentioned earlier, many of you may have been ignorant of the presence of your gift and therefore have, by default, been operating in the negative polarity of your gifts. The gifts are powerful undoubtedly, but they are equally as powerful when operating on the opposite end of them. Remember this; your gift is always there, it is a part of your make up, however, there is a huge possibility that it has been lying dormant. It may be overtaken by stress in your life, problems at home, work issues or pain from your past, but rest assured, it is ALWAYS there, you just have to find the strength and the courage to wake it up. Let's explore some of the behaviors in opposition to your gifts that may have been stagnating you from operating in your fullest potential.

Our first gift that we examined, was our beautiful gift of Intuition. Remember, intuition is the direct perception of truth independent of any reasoning process, it is keen and quick insight into a situation. In short, it is knowing without knowing how you know...sound confusing? I can almost bet that it doesn't, why? Because it has happened to each and every one of us at one point or another. We have all had access to this gift in any given moment, and we have all used it for our benefit at some point. This is the gift that shows us things to come and opens our eyes with more awareness to what *is* going on around us presently. It is the small voice that alerts us of impending danger, and even signals us when something is off with a friend or a mate. This is a gift that is spiritual and hovers in a realm that is not physical, it is energy, Spirit, vibrations and it reveals to us on an energetic level. The information perceived from this gift is rarely based on any form of physicality, it is purely spiritual. This is why it is so important to operate in the positive of this gift as opposed to its counterpart.

Let's talk about its counterpart...The opposite of your gift of Intuition would be Paranoia. Paranoia is a state in which you possess baseless and excessive suspicion of the motives of others. The precept of intuition is that it is information gained without an actual physical basis or physical evidence, so paranoia works in the exact same manner as intuition but its focus is on the negative. People who use their intuition effectively, use it to obtain pertinent information about their lives, feel out things to come, and uses its guidance to make important and even not so important decisions. Those who switch to paranoia, become suspicious at MOST things. They feel as though everyone and everything is out to get them. They may question the motive of everything, question their circumstance and place blame or deflect on anything even God. Paranoia is based on baseless information so there is truly no basis in *why* you are doing what you are doing, but you cannot bring yourself to stop because in your *mind* there IS a reason. This paranoia is created by your fears. Fears that live in your mind based on past experiences and past hurts. It will cause you to "see" things that aren't there, and feel things based on preconceived notions. In your mind, these things are real and you begin to act accordingly. Paranoia will cause you to suspect things that aren't truly there and cause you to become suspicious of the people closest to you. It is paranoia that will cause you to snoop, invade someone's privacy, go through phones, look through pockets, take a peek at emails or text messages and to become suspicious of those you think may hurt you.

Many times, women who suffer with this feel as though it is their intuition at work, this cannot be farther from the truth. Intuition does not call for the behavior that paranoia does. Intuition grants you a slight nudge of what may be coming, gives you a sneak peek into the lives of others and is what gives you that small stomach drop when there may be danger present. It does not cause immense fear, cause frantic, crazy behavior, or push rash decisions. It is small and still, it is soft and nudging, and it does not have its basis in your feelings at all. The funny thing about Paranoia and Intuition is they operate on the same *basic* premise, they both operate by giving impulses with fact less and baseless information but be very careful that you are not mistaking one for the other. Many are operating in paranoia thinking that they are using their Intuition to gain information. The two look similar but they are very much different. Ask yourself a few questions when feeling suspicious of something or someone; Did this suspicion come from a past experience? Has the person given me reason to suspect them? Am I just afraid of a particular experience happening to me again? These thoughts can all feed your paranoia and cause it to grow into an untamable monster that has the potential to wreak havoc and take over your life. Check it at the door and do not feed it by acting on your paranoid impulses. This will cause it to eventually shrink away and your true intuition can begin to move to the forefront.

Our next gift that we spoke upon was our natural gift of Nurturing. This gift is awesome in that we cultivate and take care of the things around us. We assist in the growth and supportive process of our children, our mates and at times, even our parents or co-workers. This gift is super natural to us and is simply embedded into our nature as women. The issue that arises with this gift is when we operate in the negative of it. The premise of this gift is that we offer support and provide nourishment, feed, train and educate. When these gifts shift and are given out of context or without proper motive they can turn into the other side of the gift and I will call this NAGGING. Nagging is basically to annoy with persistent faultfinding, complaints or demands. It is complaining in an irritating, wearisome, or relentless manner. Surely you can understand how having a natural desire to help, train or educate can shift into pushing someone to do what YOU want them to do. At the core of this nagging is the authentic desire to assist, but what it ends up doing is irritating and annoying those around you. It is okay to want to help, but it is not okay to begin to push, prod, force, aggravate and disturb others to do what you feel is best just because *you* feel that way. This will end up ultimately pushing those closest to you, away from you. This will upset you because your reason for behaving this way is simply because you care, it is your approach that needs work. Nagging simply means that you are relentless in finding fault and complaints, I'm sure you can see how this can push even the most loyal person away from you. Work on balancing your need to assist, help and support with doing so in a calm, positive and loving manner. If your gift is not utilized in this manner it will inevitably switch to nagging and in conclusion will give you the opposite of the results that you are pursuing.

Now we can delve right into our influential gift of Persuasion. Remember persuasion means to prevail on a person to do something, as by advising or urging". It means to induce someone to believe by appealing to reason or understanding. It means simply... to convince. Manipulation being very similar is the opposite side of the spectrum, it means to manage or influence skillfully; especially in an unfair manner. Manipulation runs very close to persuasion except in most cases you are using it for your own selfish gain. The idea that it is unfair means that it is not fair to the person it is being used against and the advantage falls on the manipulator. This is not the best way to use your power and it is surely not in your best interest to do so. The reason being is because at some point you will receive back what you have put out, and people will begin to do to you as you have done to them. This will not be fun for you. Manipulation, because of the fact that it is used for selfish gain, has the potential to hurt others in the process and build distrust. After some time, people will seriously begin to question your motives and even when the motive is pure it will always be second-guessed. You will have ruined the purity and authenticity of your relationships and they will undoubtedly begin to suffer at your expense. Manipulation carries with it a taste of dishonesty and connivance that is never respected, and once a person realizes that they have been manipulated they will not be exactly overjoyed about this. Persuasion, as I stated earlier, uses factual information along with your gift of attraction to get things done for you, it in no way uses trickery, dishonesty, deceit or a twisted plot to get things done. Take this into account the next time you want something to turn in your favor.

Which bring us directly to our next gift, The powerful gift of Attraction and its counterpart Seduction. Attraction means magnetic charm or fascination, to allure and entice. Seduction *almost* has the same meaning, except that it also means; to lead astray, to corrupt and draw away; as from principles, faith or allegiance. This simply means that you possess the same gift of attraction, but you use the gift for negativity instead of positivity. As we went over in the earlier chapter, the basis of magnifying your attraction is by utilizing positivity. Positivity is the magnet that supercharges your attraction, without this component your attraction lacks its dynamite power. Seduction utilizes the same gift of attraction, but it uses it in a negative manner to move a situation in a way that pleases you. We all have this ability inside of us to use but it would behoove us not to utilize it in this manner. It usually does not work out in our favor in the long run. The reason that I speak so strongly about using our gifts with integrity and positivity is because of the Law of Cause and Effect, we will always reap what we have sown. If we do not desire something to be done to us, then it is in our absolute best interest to not do so unto others. It will always boomerang back into your life and you will always feel the effects of what you have done to someone else whether you realize that you have done it or not. This is why it is of upmost importance to treat others as you wish to be treated and do not deviate from this law. It will work in your best interest in the future. Do not use your female powerful magnetic attraction, to lure someone off of their course, get them to switch allegiance or to sway something in your favor for narcissistic reasons, this will only swing back around to bite you in the butt when you least expect it. Always carry yourself with esteem and integrity and The Universe will always compensate you accordingly. This is also Spiritual Law.

You may notice that I am not getting very deep into the negative polarity of our gifts and there is a significant reason for this. I do not give negativity much power. It only has the power that we allow, so my job is to give you the information, let you know exactly how you may have been operating in its counterpart and move on. Once you realize what the counterpart is, it will be much easier to recognize when you may be walking in that in the future. It will be easier to "see" your behavior and to change it at will. This is also a part of your power!

Our next magnificent gift that we need to explore its counter is our gift of Passion. I am speaking on powerful and compelling emotion, strong feeling and desire. As we spoke of this gift, we talked about how powerful our emotions are and how we can use them positively. The other end of this gift would be Reckless Abandonment, Irrationality or Impetuous. Our God-given emotions are powerful and they are the ultimate catalyst in manifestation. They assist our thoughts in becoming tangible reality for us and they have the power to uplift others as well. The problem with emotions come in, when you begin to allow your negative thoughts to take over your emotions and begin to act them out without regard. Our emotions are powerful and if not reigned in they can cause catastrophic results for you. The moment that you begin acting out in your emotions you can ruin the relationships and opportunities that mean the most to you. We have all been in a situation where we have seen a person act out emotionally and how it may not have ended with the best results for them. This can happen frequently. If you are not a person who has a handle on your emotions, you may have outburst of anger, jealous rants and involve yourself in physical violence. This is NEVER good and it will never end up with a positive result. Please understand, our happy and positive emotions are what draw in and magnetize for us, the moment we begin acting out in negative emotions, what we desire will always be withheld from us. It is a repellant for good things to happen in our life. This is Spiritual Law!

Our last gift that we will discuss in this segment is our incredible gift of Communication. As we spoke about earlier, some women are better at this than others for the simple fact of personality differences, but in general we have the gift of gab. This is due partly to the fact that we move between both sides of our brains, giving us the opportunity to access information from either side in any given moment. This is an awesome and highly effective gift for the simple fact that our words are extremely powerful and create our outside world for us. This makes our communication and the words that we speak VERY IMPORTANT! Even the Bible tells us that "death and life are in the power of the tongue". Our words hold so much creation power for our lives. This is why it's counterpart is so dangerous which is Gossip and Idle Conversation. These two things are killers to you and the word around you. Our conversation as women should be uplifting, encouraging and positive. This is what will produce the best results for your life. When you stray from these and begin to creep into the lure of gossip and idle conversation, this is surely the devil's playground. These two horror shows will suck the positivity out of your life and also sabotages other's lives in the process. Gossip tears down many people in its travels and you will also be one of them as the person spreading it. It is like an infectious disease that spreads to whomever comes into contact with it and three people are ALWAYS affected, it causes harm to the listener, the victim as well as the culprit. Many feel that if the information they are speaking of is truth, it cannot be considered gossip. This cannot be farther from the truth. Gossip is idle conversation or rumors especially about the personal or private affairs of another. Just because something has truth or validity does not necessarily mean that it should be shared. Idle talk is also surely a playground for trouble. It causes destruction to many parties concerned. This gift of communication is supposed to be used for encouraging others and lifting one another up. It should be utilized for healing and affirmations, not the affairs of another. I know that we have all been guilty of engaging in this at one point or another, but it is in our best interest to steer very clear of this. We can all admit that we would surely not be pleased if we were on the other side of the gossip. This gift is powerful because our words create. They can bless our lives or curse our lives. The choice is yours.

3

<u>The Quality of a Queen</u>

When you think of the word "Queen" What is the first thing that comes to mind? When I think of the word, the first words that come to the forefront of my mind are Royalty, Regal, Etiquette, Class, Respect, Heiress, Legacy, Crown, Lineage, and a host of others but far too many to name. Queens, even from the beginning of time carry themselves in such a way that they command respect without saying a word. They do not have to beg, or showcase who they are...their crown says it all. Their behavior and demeanor tells a story and this is the story that we as women, royalty or not, need to tell as well.

There is a certain manner in which a Queen carries herself and I think it would do much good if we adopted some of these practices ourselves. There is a certain demeanor that she possesses that basically tells the world that she is royalty. These qualities range from her cleanliness, her walk, her presence, her attitude, her etiquette, her class, her appearance, how she carries herself and the list goes on. As time has moved on we have long thrown away certain principles and reduced ourselves to fads and trends and true womanhood has gone by the wayside. Think about it, it was not until the year 1920 that women were granted the right to vote and it was at that time that we were just beginning to gain the respect that we deserve as women and as equals. Women at that time carried themselves with a level of respect and dignity that we have lost somewhere along the way. We were granted our right to vote, treated as equals, allowed in the workforce with men, allowed to play professional sports, granted the rights to make equal pay, and became super independent as the women's movement crept its way in very strongly in about the 1970's. As the women became more accepted in addition to more independent, men begin subtly stepping down in compensation for it. This cycle caused women to step up even more so and as we walk into 2017, we have a society that is lacking male authority, homes without fathers, chivalry had died, females out of control using their bodies for power, and it has become cool and accepted for women to act almost identical in nature to men. We have almost completely lost and or reversed our role in society. This causes a ripple effect. Our *true* needs as a woman are not being met because we have lost true femininity and men have taken a step back from truly acting as men and gentlemen. This has caused women to become resentful, hardened, masculine and ultimately to lose respect for men in general.

This is a cycle that may or may not be broken as a society, but the way to incite general change is by first changing yourself. You can begin, once again, to walk in your femininity, to carry yourself like a lady, to walk into a room and your presence alone commands respect and literally pulls the gentleman like behavior out of a man. This is amazing power and we can begin to utilize this power on a daily basis. There are many ways to carry yourself like royalty and to keep your dignity and respect and even more so, begin to earn the respect that you require. There are also ways to carry yourself that will achieve the complete opposite. Let's explore some Queen like behavior and traits as well as what *may not* be considered Queen like.

- **Cleanliness-** This is first and foremost. Cleanliness is next to Godliness. When have you ever seen a Queen or a woman of stature and respect that is not clean? The answer is very seldom or never. How you treat your physical body is a reflection of how you treat yourself in general. Self-Love is the first step to attracting others that love you and it starts with a nice, clean fresh smelling body. No one wants to get close to a woman who is not fresh and does not value herself enough to wash up. This shows lack of respect for yourself and others around you. It only takes a few extra moments to take the time out to bathe every day in addition to cleaning your nails and hair. Being clean and well-groomed shows that you take pride in your appearance and how you present yourself to the world. Poor hygiene is not the trait of a Queen; it is the trait of a peasant. I know this sounds harsh, but it is the God's honest truth, you cannot expect people to value you and treat you with respect if you do not implement this small rule in your life. This was a ritual in the life of a Queen. Before a woman was presented to her husband, she was bathed, scrubbed with salts and fragrant oils, massaged and beautified. This went on for about seven days... after her marriage this ritual did not stop, this is the way the Queen of those days lived. This was her normalcy. Try this at home! It feels wonderful to submerge your body into a nice hot bath! Add milk, bath salts or fragrant oils. Exfoliate your body to rid it of dead skin cells and to rejuvenate your energy field. Energize your body and your Spirit by healing it with the power of water and make it a point to love on your body while you are lathering it with soap. Once you get out, make it a point to cream your body with a nice lotion or body butter, feel how soft your skin feels and appreciate the vessel that God has placed you in. This in itself will raise your vibration to regal status. The love that you exude onto yourself will most definitely be reciprocated by others as well. Trust me! Try it! It works.

- **Body Language-** Body language is key if you want to carry yourself like royalty. The key in having positive body language is feeling and being positive. You cannot have good posture and great body language if you have a negative attitude or are down and depressed. These signals will showcase throughout your body and people will be able to read them. They will be picked up by those around you and people will respond accordingly. Someone who knows who they are and knows their purpose here on this earth walks with an air of confidence that cannot be denied. When speaking of this, I am talking about confidence in who you are and what you offer the world, what I am in NO way encouraging is cockiness or arrogance, these are qualities that will turn people off and cause people to shun and dismiss your message, whatever that message may be, because of your pompous attitude. This will not serve you in the long run. Your body language should be one of love and charisma, one of openness and confidence, one of poise and assurance and last but certainly not least one of servanthood. People that are willing to serve hardly come off as negative or haughty, they possess a sense of humbleness no matter what their stature. This is the posture that you want to emit. This will ultimately cause success and these qualities alone will assist you in sending a bodily message of positivity in which you will be received well by most that you come in contact with.

- **Appearance-** Let's talk a little bit about how you present yourself to the world. Presentation is important based on how you want to be perceived and first impressions are lasting. How are you being perceived based on how you dress? Queens do not have to show off body parts to get attention, they can be fully dressed and still COMMAND attention. There is nothing wrong with dressing a little sexy but when that sexy turns into raunchy or distasteful, you are definitely sending out a certain signal. As a woman, you always want to send out the subliminal signals based on what you would like

59

to achieve, do not send out a signal that is not in agreement or alignment with what you want. This little bit of information will take you very far. Clothes should always be clean and neat and it is becoming when you present your best to the world. This can be done very simply, by taking pride in how you look. When you look good, you feel good and vice versa. This can work wonders for your self-confidence. Looking good on a regular basis tells the world that you take pride in yourself, and it can help draw more opportunities your way. There is always something professional that is emitted out when your clothing looks good. This does not mean that you have to wear expensive items or designer clothes, it simply means that clothing should fit well, be clean, neat, look good, and fit your personal style. This will undoubtedly assist you in attracting the opportunities that you desire to come your way. Opportunities will not come knocking your door down when you are in public with pajama pants, hair rollers or a bonnet. This is a fact.

- **Language-** I know this may sound far-fetched and possibly even outdated, but the way that we speak and the language that we use is important. I am not speaking of dialect or accent as much as I am the language that you choose to use. I know that as we enter into the year 2017 it is very accepted and can even be seen as cool or popular to use foul language and talk down to people, however, I am here to tell you that although it may be acceptable in the privacy of your own home or amongst friends it is not so becoming when used in public and can also be taken as offensive and rude when used in conversation with others, especially those that you do not know very well or business associates. It sends an impression that you may have a limited vocabulary or that you lack education. We all know that this is probably not the case, as I myself have even let out a few curse words every now and then, however it is wise to use discretion when hurling out swear words in the midst of professional and elders.

They may not take lightly to your language and it may also send the wrong impression of you. When you are educated, intelligent, articulate, and well- spoken, you have the ability to communicate effectively and swear words are usually not necessary. Limit them in your vocabulary or reserve them for close family and friend moments. This will serve you for the best.

- **Communication-** This brings us to our next point...communication. As a Queen, communication is very important as I stated in earlier text because our words are filled with power. We have the power to chop someone down or lift someone up. We can edify, uplift, support and encourage with our words alone. As a woman, we can be of great value to the lives around us and exhort them to be better human beings by our encouragement alone. Again, let's stay away from gossip and negative talk, this only brings people down and lowers the vibrations in the atmosphere. This is lower level behavior.

- **Confidence-** Confidence is key when it comes to walking with the air of a Queen. Confidence is not something that you can borrow from someone else, it has to come from the inside. Have you ever noticed (well of course you noticed!) that person that just exudes confidence, sensuality and charisma? They walk into a room and everyone looks up, everyone notices this person no matter what their prior focus was. This person takes pride in their attitude and demeanor, they smile, they are not shy, are open and fluid, they move with ease across a crowded room, they love everyone and they love themselves. You may ask the question "how do they do it?" This question is very common and the answer to this question is... they are not "doing" it they "ARE" it. They are not being sexy, they ARE sexy, they are not acting confident, they ARE confident. They aren't acting. They actually ARE everything they are exuding! The next question you may ask is "How do I possess that?" The answer to this question is quite simple as well...BE THAT! The first step in exuding this confidence is self-love as we stated earlier. Self-Love in a way that most people are not quite used to. Most people sacrifice their health and time for the nurturing of someone else, kids, bosses, lovers, mates, begin to take priority before the nurturing of you. The very first component in confidence is the love of oneself. Do things to begin to activate this love. Take time out for yourself and your interests, treat yourself to time off, quiet time and things of this nature. This is an imperative step to exuding this attractive energy that we seek. The next step is to work on your attitude. If you are exercising self-love, a healthy attitude begins to emanate from the inside. You are more relaxed, calm and carefree. You do not worry about what others think of you, you love yourself enough to compensate for the possible lack. This individual stays positive even in the face of negativity. You realize that your positivity is alluring. This is your true key to confidence!

- **Health-** Health is a vital element for success in your life. What is success and financial gain without a healthy body to enjoy it? You can have all of the success and financial freedom in the world but with a sick or deteriorating body, you would not be able to enjoy that freedom or very long. A healthy body, first and foremost is the highest prerequisite to success in every way shape or form. The moment that you begin to take better care of yourself mentally, emotionally and physically, your appearance, vitality and energy levels automatically take a turn or the better. You will not only look better but you will feel better as well, emanating a higher level of self-love and confidence. Keeping your body healthy is of extreme importance, because once the body begins to deteriorate it is difficult to return to its proper functioning. Take inventory of the things going on in your life, are you stressed out? Anxious?

Worrysome? These things are a strong catalyst to aged skin, low energy levels, sleepiness, and the eventual breakdown of vital organs and cells. How is your exercise regimen? How is your sex life? Is it frequent, virtually non-existent, or somewhere in-between? These two things are imperative to your health, they both release tons of natural chemicals to the body ie: Endorphins, Dopamine, Serotonin, and the list goes on. These chemicals assist in our stress relief, health and overall happiness so to speak. Our bodies tell us AND the world a story, what is yours saying? Great health is most definitely the quality of a Queen.

Queenship is an important lesson that I feel women must learn. There is a certain air to carrying yourself like a queen and it commands respect. Queens rule and reign their kingdoms with poise and dignity, and that is exactly what women should be aspiring to, ruling and reigning their personal kingdoms with this same poise and dignity. Queens are not impatient, frantic or frazzled and they are prepared for what comes their way.

They are healthy and treat their bodies with respect. Their bodies are ritualized with the finest salts and butter to soften and smooth their skin. They are well versed and intelligent and prepared for a King. They are respectful and know how to make important decisions when necessary. Queens walk with their head held high knowing who they are and the position they hold. They have nothing to prove and they don't waste time in foolish or ignorant disputes based on ignorance. Queens are poised, well-kept and take pride in their appearance. They are educated, well-rounded and approach their king with respect. They do not get irate and over-run with emotion. They take bad news in stride and put together a plan to get through it. They are prosperous and wealthy in all areas of their life and they are a blessing to others.

QUEENS! This is what you should aspire to as a woman. You may have a household to run, children to attend to and a husband that needs taken care of. You may work, own a business or engage in a lot of social activities, whatever your personal situation is, you should aspire for greatness. Do not belittle yourself by gossiping, fighting, and entering into foolish disputes, rise above what is beneath you. Stay confident in yourself, knowing who you are and what you offer the world. Take time out to read and become versed on things of intelligence. Pray, meditate and clear your mind of unwanted worry and negativity, this is not the trait of a Queen, it is unnecessary and does not serve your highest good. As a woman, you should be edifying one another and lifting each other up when down. Take great care of your health and your physical body and work on your emotional state as well while you are going through the process. Your emotional state being in balance is a very important and attractive state as a woman. No one wants to do be around or do business with an emotionally erratic and out of sort's individual. Take time out for yourself and work on your emotional, spiritual, mental, and physical healing. Time out for yourself is a very important part of this process and begin to tune into yourself for clarity and restoration in all areas. Becoming Queenlike is not a difficult process, it takes self-awareness and the power to rise above situations and recognize them for what they are. It takes the process of walking in your higher self and letting ego fall by the wayside. This will continue to awaken you so that you may walk in this stature on a daily and consistent basis.

The Queen Code

4

<u>Fun House Mirrors</u>

Let's talk about fun house mirrors for a minute or two. Have you ever been to a carnival or amusement park and entered into one of the fun houses? They can be loads of fun, but they can also be quite creepy. The mirrors can be intensely deceiving and you may find yourself dizzy and floundering around looking for the way out. This is meant for jest and none other, however, this would not be amusing at all if this were a situation in your real world. Could you imagine going on and about in your life with a bunch of distorted mirrors in a maze that only has one exit? Well, guess what my friend, this is the world that we live in every day! Fun house mirrors are indeed a reality for some of us. The premise of these mirrors at this carnival or park is to trick the mind and confuse you so that you do not find a way out. Of course, as I stated earlier, this is for fun and fun only but when this is what begins to occur in your reality, it is not much fun at all and can be damaging to your life.

Fun house mirrors are your perception and everyone around you has a different one. Let me give you an example; there can be two people in the same room at exactly the same time, looking at the same thing and actually "see" or interpret something totally different. I am going to explain how this works... We are all operating out of our own personal filters or lenses so to speak. These filters are put in place by many things ie: our upbringing, religion, social conditioning, past experiences, as well as our present situations. These differences in everyone's life causes them to see things differently by default. The differences can be big or small but they will never be exactly alike between individuals. This is usually where any type of confusion or conflict can set in as it relates to misunderstandings or misconstrued outlooks.

With the understanding of this key fact, it should be much easier to take it easy on our fellow sisters, it should be much easier to be less judgmental, and angry when someone opposes us or makes a decision that we do not quite agree with or even more so, don't understand.

The Queen Code

This is what will separate you from the average to walk
in your true divinity. The understanding of one another
is imperative if you want to live in harmony without
bickering or exhibiting hate over menial disputes. It is
not okay nor is it becoming to operate in pettiness
because of a difference in opinion or lifestyle. This is
where I feel that women can use the most work. It is
our perceptions of situations that can get us into the
most trouble, especially as it relates to other women or
our significant other. Perceptions play a very big and
important role in how we interpret a situation, this is
where working on our attitudes and thought processes
come into play. Remember, when you think negatively,
you feel negatively and act out as a result of those
feelings. There can be many situations that you may
have misread based on "where you are" at the moment.
When I say "where you are" I am speaking of, where
you are emotionally, physically, economically, spiritually
and even mentally. You will always be at different
stages in these areas based on where you are in your
life at the moment or even more so where you have
been. Take for instance; You could have grown up in a
household very privileged. Things came to you easily

and without much effort. You may have had a supportive family and never truly had to want or struggle for anything, everything may have been effortless for you and you were truly blessed. On the other hand, you may have grown up in a poor, or abusive household. Things that others take for granted may have been super hard to come by for you, you may not have had the support that you needed whether financially or emotionally and you may have walked through life feeling alone until you became of age. Take these two very different lives and put them in the same exact scenario, let's say an opportunity for a job, or they may just meet a handsome man at the mall. These two women will have two very different responses to what is occurring. Let's take the example of the job opportunity; the woman who had the effortless life will more than likely walk into this situation with an unmatched positivity. She will feel as though nothing can stand in her way and basically the job is hers before she even interviews for it. She will have an air of confidence when she walks into the room and she will ultimately believe that nothing can be withheld from her. This will ultimately cause more opportunities to come her way based simply upon the fact of her perception and confidence. Let's take a look at the other woman who did not have such a fortunate upbringing. This woman may hear about the job opportunity and second guess herself immediately, she may feel as though everyone else has a better chance than she has, she will walk into the room defeated before they even deny her and she may send off signals that will push away the opportunity that she truly wants. This is unfortunate but this is what I speak of when I talk about perception being different based on certain factors. Let's explore the two women when they meet this handsome man at the mall. Our second woman will see this man, and although she may have had a not so lovely past, she may have tried her best to get over it and learn to love and trust again, she has grown emotionally and mentally and attempted to start over, she meets this man and they have great conversation and begin to date. She is truly happy with him, however, it is only a matter of time before "what she sees" is jaded if she has not *truly* gotten over the pain of her past. She may become suspicious, she may desire an obscene amount of attention based on the attention and affection that she lacked growing up or in her past. She may feel alive and supported every time he tells her he loves her only to do things that will ultimately push him away in the long run. This is not to say that she has to stay this way forever, but she has some inner work to do before her outlook on situations or circumstances may indeed change. This is what perceptions or your outlook can do to you. Please remember, this does not always have to do with a negative sense, I just need you to realize that perception plays a big part in our lives overall.

People's behavior, almost without exception is determined by perception. It is wise to understand that studies show that the average person's conversation is negative, so you can see based on this fact alone, how people can come to negative conclusions based on their perceptions. The key here is choosing your thoughts once information is processed and perceived...for example; you can walk into a room, everyone in a group that was engaged in conversation suddenly stops and looks up at you. You have two choices here, you can choose to believe that this group of people were engaged in conversation about *you* hence their abrupt halt when you arrived or you can choose to believe that you look beautiful today and everyone looked up because *you* entered the room, the choice is yours. You do not always have to perceive a situation as negative, ESPECIALLY when there is no proof of the negativity. Beware of the tendency to read into things that are not there or vain assumptions, this is a surefire way to enter the road to defeat and depression. Assumptions will never ever put you on the right track, especially negative ones, negative assumptions will turn into a belief, and with belief comes expectation. When you believe something, you expect something and then you act accordingly, very simple. If you watch the 6pm news the night before and the weather reporter states that it will rain the next evening, if you believe that weather reporter, you will act out on the expectation of that rain whether it be by changing or postponing plans or even something as simple as bringing your umbrella or dressing accordingly. This is how belief works. Once you believe something, you begin to prepare for it. The example that I gave is in relation to the physical...something obvious, however this works in the same manner as it relates to the unobvious. Don't assume there is negativity going on when there is no proof that there is negativity going on, when there is no *"proof"*, you have the innate ability to change what you have perceived in your mind and you can literally change your thought about a situation to produce a different result. It's important to realize that your thoughts about a situation produces your feelings and this is what changes your vibrations, so when people are around you and you feel that they may be standoffish or aloof as it relates to you, check out the vibes that you may be sending out as well, as it turns out, *you* may actually end up being the guilty one. I'm just saying!

Perceptions are the filters in which we see the world. They are our lenses to which we see through, some are tainted, foggy, rose colored, clear, smudged, dirty, sunny etc. Whatever the particular lens it is that you are working with, at times it may be need to be cleaned or wiped off for you to see a situation clearly and you can do this by evaluating FACTS not assumptions. The true meaning of perception is "The act of apprehending by means of the senses or mind" All this means is that you gain information in your mind based on your senses or understanding of a situation and as we addressed earlier, this can be very different for everybody. There are many examples where your perception plays a part in your everyday life. Let's look at this: You have been cheated on in the past, your husband is planning you a surprise party, you have no idea about this party, but his days at work have been surprisingly longer and he has been having quiet phone conversations behind your back. Although this man has never shown you anything but love and you have no reason to believe otherwise, you are convinced of the fact that he is having an affair. You sense something is off, but can't place what it is. In reality he is preoccupied with planning your party, but you can't seem to see past the fact that he could be cheating based on your past experiences. Another example; You may have been having a hard time at work lately, you have simply been preoccupied with stress at home and your work performance has taken a hit. Your boss comes over to you and tells you that he needs to set up some time to speak with you, immediately your mind may go to the fact that he is going to let you go, when in reality, once you get into his office he explains to you that he notices you have been a little off and he wants to know if he can be of support in any way... You see, this is what perception does, it filters the information that we receive with what we already have in our minds. A lot of things that we think we see or feel, are not even really there, they are literally figments of our imagination!

Once you see that your perceptions determine your behavior, you can immediately begin to shift your focus from your actions to your attitude and watch things change for the better. I read in a book "The 24 Hour Turn-Around" That once you change with your mind's eye, you will begin to see things differently with your physical eye. Situations will not seem as bad or haunting, you can get rid of assumptions completely, and you can see things as they TRULY are and not have to filter them through your past pain, hurt or betrayals. Learn to look at a situation for what it is, and always, always try to think the best even when the evidence looks otherwise. This will serve YOU in the grand scheme of things.

5

<u>The Crown Stays Put</u>

Our crowns represent something important. We know that we do not wear a literal crown, but our lifestyle, our mentality, thought processes, and even actions represent our crown. How we present ourselves to the world and the morals, standards and ethics by which we live by are also our crowns. These are important and it separates the women from the little girls. There is a distinct difference between the behavior of a WOMAN and the behavior of a little girl. We will delve more into this later...however let's talk about what our crown represents. As a woman, this crown represents Who we are, Our Divinity, Our femininity, Our power, Our value, Our standards, and Our kingdoms. We are divine creatures by right and we have amazing powers as we covered in our beginning chapter. This crown is important, it sends a message to the world of who you are and what you are about. There are many ways to represent your crown and the idea is for people to see it and understand it without you having to broadcast it. What I mean by this is, to let your lifestyle bear witness to who you are, use words if you have to. People should see the light of who you are, they should feel the energy of your presence and they should be able to see your character even from afar. This is what I mean when I speak of representing your crown.

There are many situations that occur in your life that may cause your crown to fall off or situations that may even cause you to want to take it off and stoop lower than your character or value system. We all know of situations like this, situations that aggravate you, situations that irk you, situations that upset you and ultimately cause you to want to jump out of character. These can come up in the form of petty disputes with women, circumstances surrounding your children, dealing with ex relationships that include children, work based issues or issues with co-worker...etc. etc. It is up to you to maintain your integrity and character as it relates to any situation that angers or upsets you. None of us are exempt as it comes to matters like this and we have all fallen short of acting in perfect behavior when we feel slighted, disrespected or devalued. This is normal and I don't want you to feel guilty or disappointed in yourself if you have been acting less than becomingly, however it is up to you to begin *now* to make a shift in your behavior.

Let's talk about Queens, Queens do not stoop to the behaviors of others, Queens do not have to prove who and what they are, Queens do not have to fight for position, Queens rise above petty disputes and do not settle into that which is beneath them, Queens do not waste their day gossiping and starting chaos, and Queens do not settle for less than what they are worth and what they have rightfully earned. Queens are purposeful, they have vision and foresight, they know that which needs to be done and they complete the task, Queens hold their heads high even in the face of adversity and Queens do not give up on a dream. This is what we should aspire to! As women, we have to learn to give up the pettiness. Petty is beneath us, petty serves no purpose and petty causes trouble where there need not be trouble. It is understandable to be upset when there is an injustice served against you but it is not okay to have an eye for an eye mentality or to try to serve justice yourself just to get back at someone for hurting you. This will serve no healing purpose in the end. This will only wind up hurting both parties involved. Also recognize that once you stoop to the level of someone else, you will never feel good about it afterwards. It is almost like your internal compass lets you know that you have veered off of your path. What is Petty? I am glad that you asked! Petty is giving attention to something of little or no importance or consequence, it is a showing caused by meanness of spirit. So, in short, this means to give attention to things that mean absolutely nothing and to act out of a mean spirit. Have you ever been in the presence of a petty person? Did you notice how every little thing bothers them or sets them off and how they choose to address it? A petty person will be upset if they walk into a room and *one* person does not speak to them, a petty person will look at a gift given to them and compare it with a gift given to someone else, a petty person will be hurt by someone and instead of going to that person, will set themselves on a fire blaze to gossip and destroy them. Understand that petty people do petty things and operate on a petty level. This is not where you want to be. When you notice petty things that means that is the level from which you resonate. I know It sounds harsh and no one wants to hear this, but look at it in this frame of mind; a Queen will not notice the same things a peasant would. Its tight but it's right! You will not even notice the smaller things if this is not where your head is at in the first place. It takes a small minded person to notice small minded things...If this is you, it is okay! Just begin to set your mind on the bigger pictures in life. Set your mind on goals for yourself, your family and your household. Set intentions on where you want to be and the growth that you want to see within yourself. This is where being petty will have to see its way out. When you are focused on the bigger and the more important things in life, you truly don't have the time or the mind to focus on the small stuff. When you have a bigger focus, you will not go looking for subliminal messages on Facebook, you will not notice the person who did not say "Hello" when you walked into a room, you not care about the gossip that is floating around about you, you will not give energy to the woman you feel disrespects you and your relationship, you will not have an eye for an eye mentality, understanding that the laws of the Universe work whether we are aware of them or not and you will surely not let the behavior of others get to you or alter your behavior. Trust me, this works...I speak from personal experience. Petty is not the way to go, it will offer you nothing positive in the long run. It causes you to stoop to a level that you should not even be on in the first place. Let me share with you a personal example; I usually pride myself on not being petty and rising above most menial situations. I like to look at all sides and I pride myself on making an unbiased decision even if that decision includes my own circumstance. Well anyway, this is my story... I am married and I had just had my last son who was about six months old at the time. I was breastfeeding and I think I may have had a slight bout of postpartum depression, I just didn't feel like myself and this went on for a while. I kept telling my husband that I needed him and wanted him to spend more time with me, I was not being dramatic, I *really* needed him, his energy, his talks, his hugs, his love and compassion, but every day he left early and each and every night he would return home late. I had the responsibility of ALL of the children including a 1.5 year old that he had from another relationship. Stressed out was not even the word for what I was going through. Night after night he would return home late, and if he did come home early, he would eat and promptly leave the house again only to return even later. Well as fate had it, one particular night, I was super excited, he had actually come home at a decent hour; by decent, I mean an hour in which I was still awake and we could have talked or watched a movie or something. NOPE! He came in, ate his dinner that **I prepared** for him, drank a glass of wine, got into the shower and left. I was truly hurt. He did not care about my needs at all. So, what did I do? I decided to take a ride to where I thought he may be. Lo and Behold! He was exactly where I thought he was! He was at his daughter's mothers house. I did not have a problem with that per se, they have a child together, but what I did have a HUGE problem with, was the fact that we have a horrible history with that situation and I had just told him that I needed him and here he was giving attention to someone else, someone else who I felt had no respect for our relationship in the first place, nor did he. I had seen enough! Lol, I took a drive to my best friend's house... WAIT! It gets even better! My friend was eight months pregnant and SUPER hormonal! She gave me the worst advice ever, she told me to go back over there and to fight for what I wanted. She told me that I was always backing down and for once I needed to stand up for myself, fight for what I wanted and deserved and let him know that I was not going to tolerate any more hurt. For some STRANGE reason, based on where my mind was at the time, this sounded like a good idea. Although, it went against everything that I stood for and went against how *I would have normally* handled it, at that moment, it actually sounded perfect! So we set out together to this woman's house. (You can tell how this was a bad idea already) I get out of the car and we walk to her door, all the while plotting a strategy to get him outside. Finally, my friend tells me to knock on the door because I NEED ANSWERS! As I was walking to the door, I chickened out and began to try to walk the other way and told her I would just deal with it when he got home. Once again, she yells "Its 2AM!!" Why wouldn't you want answers NOW! So as I am walking away, she decided to knock on the door. Oh God! It was too late to run, I had to just stand my ground. My husband opened the door, and looked at me with a look that said "What are you doing here?" I just looked at him and said "So this is what you are up to?" He looked at me angrily, looked down at his clothes, and says "I'm fully dressed" At that moment I could not take anymore and I hit him in the face! He grabbed my arm, I hit him again and again and we tousled our way into an empty grassy knoll where we kept tousling and arguing while my friend and his daughter's mother watched. It was a CRAZY emotionally charged moment for me and I had never felt that much anger and fire cursing through my body as I did that night. At that moment, he had totally lost my respect and in that same moment I think I lost his as well. We had a horrible breakup with him telling me to leave, and I left our house and started a new life, however, deep, deep down in my Spirit, I knew that I could have handled that situation better based on **who I am!** Now, I know that most reading this are saying "Well, he should not have been over there at 2am, that's disrespectful!" to which I would absolutely agree, however it does not give me a right to disrespect him because he disrespected me...understand? Your behavior should never be based on another's behavior but for the betterment of you. There was a better, more mature, more respectful way to handle that without embarrassing and humiliating myself in the middle of the night smack dab in the middle of an apartment complex a complex that I did not even live at and my aunt lived next door! I could have waited until he returned home to deal with it and even if I decided that I no longer wanted the relationship, I could have simply expressed that fact and made my moves to leave. It did not have to turn out as catastrophic as it did. I realized that I had to own my part in the situation and forgave myself for acting out of my usual character and for taking my crown off or allowing it to be knocked off in that moment. Yes, he could have done some things differently as well, but it is not my job to point out what he did wrong or what I feel was wrong, it is my job to look at MY part and to ultimately work on me. So even after I allowed my crown to fall off, once I acknowledged what I could have done things differently, acknowledged my wrong and the part that I played, I kindly picked my crown back up, straightened it on my head, and walked away with my head held high, knowing that Queens make mistakes too.

It was *that* thought that kept me going and allowed me to forgive myself for acting so much out of character. I even more so had to deal with the anger at myself for allowing someone to get me to stoop so low! How dare I give someone that much power and control over my life and my outcome! How dare I allow someone or a situation to get so much under my skin that it caused me to humiliate *myself?* I did not like that at all and I vowed to myself to never allow a situation to pull me to such a sinking level ever again. This is what I speak of when I say, no matter what your actions are, when you are acting petty, you will never truly feel good about your actions once it is all said and done. Do not act out in petty anger, you may not be able to take back what you have done and it may end up affecting that person forever just because you made a decision based on being small minded. We are so much better than that, we are so much smarter than that, and we are so much more divine than that.

If I can close this with one important point; it will be to NEVER let your crown be pulled off because of pettiness or anger, NEVER take your own crown off to get back at someone who has hurt you and NEVER let your crown slide off by gossiping and being malicious to others. This is a sure way to lose your crown and it will be hard to replace once people began to see you as a certain type of person...a person who is mean spirited, revengeful, petty, character assassinating, small-minded, or manipulative. These traits will never serve you for your highest good. This has all happened to the best of us, when someone hurts you, lies on you, betrays you, disrespects you, devalues you, humiliates you or anything else for that matter; handle it accordingly, but handle it in a way that causes you to rise above the situation and not to sink below it. Understand that God and The Universe are always at work and whatever has hurt you or done you wrong, everyone is paid out by the law of Karma, Sowing and Reaping and Cause and Effect, no one *gets away* with anything. It always comes back...Just remember that.

6

<u>Ruling Your Queendom</u>

As a woman, we all have our own personal journeys, pathways, experiences and bridges that we have to cross. We have all gone through personal experiences that had the potential to break us and possibly destroy us, this is where our strength and resilience comes from, and it is *this* strength that will keep us going along our way. This is where our personal kingdoms or queendoms comes into play. Every woman is unique and our situations, experiences and circumstances are undoubtedly unique as well. This is why it is completely up to you to keep your inner man, your spirit, your attitude, your perceptions, your families, your career and everything that has anything to do with your life and how you run it intact. This is what I mean by ruling your personal kingdom.

Many women get distracted by others and what they may have going on around them. You may be worried about things going on at the workplace, meddling in other's business, tampering in your *adult* children's lives, worried about your next relationship or when you may get one. This list can go on and on, but it is of extreme importance to concern yourself about your personal realm of influence. What this simply means is; concern yourself about the things that concern YOU. Do not waste time and precious energy concerned about the affairs of others. You have a personal kingdom that you have to reign and rule over and you have to reign and rule this kingdom successfully in order to see positive results in your life. These areas include but are not limited to; your spirituality, your physical body, your mental health, your husband and children, your career, your purpose, your personal needs, your well-being, your household, and whatever else that you hold personal responsibility for. This is your yard and your flowers that needs tending so to speak, so it is up to you to water it, cultivate it, fertilize it, prune it, and grow it. Some women have more areas that need to be tended to than others, but we all have our own gardens that need attending whether large or small. You may be a single business woman who does not have a family or children, however you still have to worry about your mental and emotional health, your career, your physical health, and your physical appearance. On the other hand, you may be a woman who does not have a career but you are a full-time mom and housewife and are involved in many extra-curricular activities... You may be a wife and mother and also still work full or part-time as well, wherever you are, you still have to make sure your personal ship stays afloat. Now the question remains; How do we do that? How do we reign our kingdoms effectively?

Well, first things first, you have to take an assessment of where you are right now. Figure out what you have on your plate, assess how you are feeling mentally, emotionally and even physically as your health plays a very significant part in this process. You have to take a good look at what you have going on in your life at the moment and figure out what it is that you may want to add or delete. Ask yourself, how are your children? Where does your relationship stand, is it good for the most part or does it need mending? Where do you wish to be as it relates to your job or career? Are you content or maybe you need to move on? Ask yourself, how are your family and interpersonal relationships? Do you have dreams and goals? Where are you as it relates to those dreams? Do you have weight loss or weight gain goals? Are you seeking a new relationship? Do you truly enjoy your life? These are the things taking place in your personal kingdom.

Once you have taken the assessment of the things taking place in your personal kingdom, it is now your role to make adjustments where necessary. At times it may be quite difficult to see where things may need fixing and this is for various reasons.

- Most times when you are in the middle of trying times, it is not easy to find your way out, this is where the assistance of a close friend, coach or counselor may need to enter the picture.

- Your focus may be elsewhere. Many times when things are off kilter in your life, it is because you have lost focus and stopped paying attention to it. You may have started to focus on things that are of less importance and the important things have ended up falling by the wayside.

- You have turned a blind eye. There are some who know exactly what is going on in their lives but for the sake of sanity, have purposely chosen not to deal with things at this time. You may feel that it is just too much work to get started and therefore have procrastinated on your progress.

- You are preoccupied. The bottom line is... you may just be too busy with work or children to really sit down to sort things out.

- You are hurting. There are times that occur in our lives where we have literally just gone through too much, more than we think we can bear and we are paralyzed in our current states and cannot move until we heal.

As we look at the various reasons for why it may be difficult to make the necessary adjustments, let us also explore the many facets in how we can rule and reign our kingdoms effectively.

- Become Aware - Don't allow distractions to get in your way. Mind your business, stay focused on what is important, which is your lifeggb and it moving in the direction that you would prefer.

- Set Goals- Setting Goals are important. They will inadvertently reveal whether you are on track or not. They keep you on task and assist in your forward movement.

- Build Yourself- Building yourself is imperative to having a positive life. It is wise to build yourself spiritually as well as mentally and emotionally. Read books, educate yourself on new concepts, attend church, bible studies or women's groups. These will all help facilitate in the allowing of yourself to evolve and grow.

- Pay Attention- Most things fall apart or come undone simply because we are not paying enough attention. There are areas in your life that you may have neglected for quite some time now due to the mere fact that you have not been paying attention or have been preoccupied with something else. This is a sure way for things to unravel and you will have no idea where it even started.

- Use Your Power- It is common for women to negate or forget that they even have power. We have awesome powers that we can use at any given moment to alter our situations for the better. Let's begin to utilize them more often than not.

- Mind Your Business- I know we have all heard the saying "Sweep around your own front door before you try to sweep around mines" This cannot be more true. It is easy to neglect your own lawn so to speak when you are busy watering your neighbors grass. Stay out of other's personal situations and focus more on your own.

These are just a few ways to get started. It is not always easy to rule and reign effectively but you have to treat your life and your world like it's your own personal organization because it IS one! It has the capability to run like a well-oiled machine or sink like a broken ship, but how it runs is entirely up to you and none other than you.

Many make the mistake of allowing others too much power in the direction that your life takes. No one should ever be allowed that type of power, there is only one captain on this ship and that captain is you. Even in the event of marriage, your personal kingdom will still reign in the area of self-care, nurturing oneself and taking good care of your body and mind. This should be without exception. If you are stressed, not feeling well or burnt out it will surely spill over into other areas of your life as well. It is your job to keep your physical and mental health up to par so that you may be effective. If you are not taking care of yourself, you cannot help take care of others, your family and career included.

Let's look at how you can rule in these two components

- CAREER- As it comes down to your career, there are many ways to rule in this area. You may have a family, you may not but if this is your focus, keep this area tight. First things first, do not allow your career to take over your life. Do not neglect things such as dating, going out or regular self- care. If you begin to do this, you will find yourself soon resenting this area of your life. Make sure that you take care of yourself and your personal needs along the way. This is extremely important. What some don't understand is that your career can be ran just like your own business. The value that you would put on running your own business should be put into your career or purpose as well. Make sure that you are doing what you love, this is imperative. If you do not love what it is that you are doing, you are fighting a losing battle. Love will give you the passion to continue on even when things are not going so well, feeling like you are working towards a goal or a purpose will ignite your fire to rise up in your passion. Take the time to educate yourself and elevate yourself higher in your field. It is one thing to go to school and obtain a degree, it is another to continue to educate yourself on your particular craft and to master it. Put your heart into what you do. If you do not have your heart in what you are doing, it will show and your work ethic and productivity will indeed suffer. When you are working for others; stay productive, arrive on time, show interest, be involved, invest yourself, and go the extra mile. These things will serve you and take you to the next level.

- FAMILY- As it relates to your household, you may have much on your plate. To rule effectively in your household, certain things should be in order. If you have a husband, or mate that resides with you, they should be taken care of, not in a mothering sense but whatever they require from you should be handled ie; support, encouragement etc. This will be different for every woman but it should not be neglected. If you have children, they should be well taken care of, fed, clean, well-behaved and supported. This should never go unnoticed or overlooked. Our children need us to be present and they need to feel supported. This is the energy that we bring to the household, a warm, loving, nurturing and supportive energy. Our home should be clean and well-kept. I myself fall short of this as well, sometimes with my busy schedule I just do not have the time to clean it, however, I do have teenage boys and as of now, I have begun to enlist their help. This is the process of delegating to others in the house to assist you as well. Have you ever been to a woman's house and it is dirty and un-kept? We all act like it is okay, but there is no surprise that we do not feel comfortable when welcomed into that home. There is certain energy that un-kept houses give out. It says that the women in charge of this home, does not care or has other priorities. I know it sounds small, but this is a big deal. The men in our lives also do not like coming home to a dirty house. If you both work, come up with a plan that he assists you in certain areas and times to clean it. This way, you will both end up happy. Another thing that I have found works is to keep your home organized. Having an organized home, meaning everything has its proper place, keeps your mind at ease. There is absolutely nothing worse than having to pay a bill or needing an important document and you have no idea where it can be because everything is strolled all over the pace. Keep your mind at rest. Organize your home as best you can and watch how you will begin to *feel* the difference.

If you are a Queen who is juggling both career and family, we salute you! You have a humungous kingdom and you are truly blessed! I know that as a woman, sometimes it feels like the entire world rests on our shoulders and at times it really does. We juggle and juggle and juggle and sometimes it can be overwhelming. We are always coming through for everyone; bosses, husbands, children, family and we will not hesitate to neglect our own needs for the sake of meeting others. I am here to tell you that this is not healthy! I know, I was the Queen of putting EVERYONE else's needs above my own. This took a toll on me and finally I broke down. Doing this will wreak havoc on your health, your appearance, your balance and ultimately your life. It is a no-go! Although the nature of this chapter is to rule and reign your personal kingdom, the most important idea that I would love for you to take home is that is all starts with SELF-CARE! If you do not take care of you, in the best way possible, you will never ever be able to take care of others or anything else for that matter. If you are not okay emotionally, mentally or even physically, you will carry this baggage with you along the way and it will affect every area of your life. We have amazing gifts and we are the nurtures of this world but we have to nurture ourselves, our Spirits and our minds of course. When you nurture your Spirit, you become strong in areas that you have previously been weak, you are able to hear that small voice that tells you that you need rest or restoration and you gain the strength to handle the things that come along your personal path. When you nurture your mind, you begin to recognize that negativity does not serve a purpose for your greater good, you gain a handle of your emotions and learn how to handle obstacles with grace and tact. This is what sets you apart as a woman. The nurturing, cultivating, evolving and growing of oneself. This separates the woman from the little girls. It takes a strong, powerful woman to grow past your hurts, your betrayals, your mishaps and your mistakes and not to bring them along for the ride of your life. It takes power and resilience to let them go, not knowing what may replace them. Work on being the BEST you that you can be and waste no time on comparisons with others. This is not a race, this is your own personal journey and your pace is your own. Try your best to rise above what has ailed you, what has come against you and what has hurt you... possibly almost beyond recognition. These experiences DO NOT define you, they are a moment in time and time is fleeting. It passes on. I want you to know inside, beyond a shadow of a doubt that you are a victor, you are special, you are an overcomer, you are strong, powerful, gifted and you have what it takes to live this life and live it victoriously if you so choose based on your decisions. You will ALWAYS make it through. This is what makes you special, this is what sets you apart and this is what makes you a Queen!

Tonisha Dawson has been leading and helping people to change their lives for over 15 years. She teaches bi-weekly courses on life changing topics, runs an interactive life coaching group and helps women to rebuild and regain their self-esteem. She holds a masters in Metaphysics, A Bachelors in Holistic Life Coaching with a focus on relationships, as well as a Certification from the National Association of Christian Counseling (NACC) as a Certified Spiritual Advisor.

Tonisha Dawson

Tonisha Dawson Coaching Therapies

Tonishadawson.com

lovetherapies@gmail.com

lovetherapies.wordpress.com

The Queen Code

CPSIA information can be obtained
at www.ICGtesting.com
Printed in the USA
BVHW040759301120
594471BV00020B/428

9 781530 617937